50 Premium Italian Pasta Recipes for the Kitchen

By: Kelly Johnson

Table of Contents

- Spaghetti alla Carbonara
- Fettuccine Alfredo
- Lasagna Bolognese
- Tagliatelle with Truffle Sauce
- Pappardelle with Wild Boar Ragu
- Penne alla Vodka
- Gnocchi di Patate with Sage Butter
- Ravioli di Ricotta e Spinaci
- Linguine alle Vongole
- Tortellini in Brodo
- Fettuccine al Pesto Genovese
- Orecchiette with Broccoli Rabe
- Cacio e Pepe
- Rigatoni alla Norma
- Fagottini di Pasta con Funghi
- Pasticcio di Maccheroni
- Spaghetti con Pomodorini e Basilico
- Farfalle with Lemon and Zucchini
- Pappardelle with Porcini Mushrooms
- Cannelloni with Ricotta and Spinach
- Spaghetti aglio, olio e peperoncino
- Gnocchi alla Sorrentina
- Lasagna alla Caprese
- Tagliatelle with Duck Ragù
- Ravioli al Nero di Seppia
- Penne all'Amatriciana
- Fusilli with Sausage and Kale
- Tagliatelle with Lobster and Saffron
- Spaghetti with Clams and Cherry Tomatoes
- Tortellini alla Panna
- Tortellini with Mushroom Cream Sauce
- Ziti al Forno with Sausage and Mozzarella
- Spaghetti alla Puttanesca
- Ravioli with Brown Butter and Sage
- Gnocchi with Gorgonzola Sauce

- Linguine with Scallops and Lemon
- Pappardelle with Truffle Cream Sauce
- Risotto alla Milanese with Pasta
- Penne alla Puttanesca
- Bucatini all'Amatriciana
- Fettuccine with Shrimp and Asparagus
- Orecchiette with Sausage and Broccoli
- Ravioli with Butternut Squash
- Cavatelli with Sweet Potatoes and Brown Butter
- Spaghetti alle Vongole Veraci
- Agnolotti with Braised Beef
- Tortellini with Parmesan Broth
- Tagliolini with Anchovies and Capers
- Lasagna di Pesce
- Pappardelle with Veal Ragù

Spaghetti alla Carbonara

Ingredients:

- 400g spaghetti
- 150g guanciale, diced (or pancetta if guanciale is unavailable)
- 4 large eggs (preferably room temperature)
- 100g Pecorino Romano cheese, finely grated
- Freshly ground black pepper
- Salt for the pasta water

Instructions:

1. Bring a large pot of salted water to a boil. Cook the spaghetti according to package instructions until al dente.
2. While the pasta is cooking, heat a large pan over medium heat. Add the diced guanciale and cook until crispy, about 5–7 minutes.
3. In a mixing bowl, whisk the eggs with the grated Pecorino Romano cheese and a generous amount of freshly ground black pepper until smooth.
4. When the pasta is cooked, reserve 1 cup of pasta water and drain the rest.
5. Add the hot pasta directly to the pan with the guanciale, tossing to coat in the rendered fat.
6. Remove the pan from heat and quickly stir in the egg mixture, tossing vigorously to create a creamy sauce. Add reserved pasta water as needed to adjust the consistency.
7. Serve immediately with extra Pecorino Romano and black pepper on top.

Fettuccine Alfredo

Ingredients:

- 400g fettuccine
- 100g unsalted butter
- 200g Parmesan cheese, finely grated
- Salt for the pasta water

Instructions:

1. Cook fettuccine in a large pot of salted boiling water until al dente. Reserve 1 cup of pasta water, then drain.
2. In a large pan over low heat, melt the butter.
3. Add the cooked fettuccine and toss to coat.
4. Gradually add the grated Parmesan, tossing to create a creamy sauce. Use reserved pasta water to adjust consistency.
5. Serve immediately, garnished with additional Parmesan if desired.

Lasagna Bolognese

Ingredients:

- 12 lasagna sheets
- 500g Bolognese sauce
- 500ml béchamel sauce
- 200g mozzarella cheese, shredded
- 100g Parmesan cheese, grated

Instructions:

1. Preheat oven to 180°C (350°F).
2. In a baking dish, spread a thin layer of Bolognese sauce. Add a layer of lasagna sheets.
3. Spread a layer of béchamel sauce, followed by Bolognese, and sprinkle with mozzarella and Parmesan.
4. Repeat layers, finishing with béchamel and a generous topping of cheese.
5. Bake for 25–30 minutes until golden and bubbling. Allow to rest for 10 minutes before serving.

Tagliatelle with Truffle Sauce

Ingredients:

- 400g tagliatelle
- 100ml heavy cream
- 50g truffle paste or truffle oil
- 50g Parmesan cheese, grated
- Salt and pepper to taste

Instructions:

1. Cook tagliatelle in salted boiling water until al dente. Reserve 1/2 cup pasta water, then drain.
2. In a large pan, heat the heavy cream over medium heat. Stir in truffle paste or truffle oil.
3. Add the cooked tagliatelle and toss to coat. Stir in Parmesan cheese and reserved pasta water as needed for a smooth sauce.
4. Season with salt and pepper to taste, and serve hot with additional Parmesan if desired.

Pappardelle with Wild Boar Ragu

Ingredients:

- 400g pappardelle
- 500g wild boar meat, diced
- 1 onion, finely chopped
- 2 carrots, finely chopped
- 2 celery stalks, finely chopped
- 2 garlic cloves, minced
- 400g canned tomatoes
- 200ml red wine
- 2 tbsp olive oil
- Salt and pepper to taste
- Fresh parsley for garnish

Instructions:

1. Heat olive oil in a large pot. Sauté onion, carrot, celery, and garlic until softened.
2. Add wild boar meat and brown on all sides.
3. Pour in red wine and simmer until reduced by half. Add tomatoes and season with salt and pepper.
4. Simmer gently for 2–3 hours until tender. Serve over cooked pappardelle, garnished with parsley.

Penne alla Vodka

Ingredients:

- 400g penne
- 2 tbsp olive oil
- 1 small onion, finely chopped
- 2 garlic cloves, minced
- 400g canned tomatoes
- 100ml vodka
- 100ml heavy cream
- 50g Parmesan cheese, grated
- Salt and pepper to taste

Instructions:

1. Cook penne in salted boiling water until al dente. Reserve 1/2 cup pasta water, then drain.
2. Heat olive oil in a pan, sauté onion and garlic until fragrant. Add tomatoes and cook for 10 minutes.
3. Pour in vodka and simmer for 5 minutes. Stir in heavy cream.
4. Add penne and toss to coat. Adjust with reserved pasta water, season with salt and pepper, and sprinkle with Parmesan.

Gnocchi di Patate with Sage Butter

Ingredients:

- 500g potato gnocchi
- 100g unsalted butter
- 6 fresh sage leaves
- Salt to taste
- Parmesan cheese for serving

Instructions:

1. Cook gnocchi in salted boiling water until they float to the surface. Drain.
2. Melt butter in a pan over medium heat. Add sage leaves and cook until fragrant.
3. Toss gnocchi in the sage butter. Serve with Parmesan cheese.

Ravioli di Ricotta e Spinaci

Ingredients:

- 400g ricotta-spinach ravioli
- 50g butter
- 1 garlic clove, minced
- 100g Parmesan cheese, grated
- Fresh nutmeg, grated
- Salt and pepper to taste

Instructions:

1. Cook ravioli in salted boiling water until al dente. Drain.
2. Melt butter in a pan, add garlic, and cook for 1 minute.
3. Toss ravioli in the butter, season with nutmeg, salt, and pepper. Sprinkle with Parmesan to serve.

Linguine alle Vongole

Ingredients:

- 400g linguine
- 500g fresh clams, cleaned
- 2 garlic cloves, minced
- 100ml white wine
- 2 tbsp olive oil
- Fresh parsley, chopped
- Salt and pepper to taste

Instructions:

1. Cook linguine in salted boiling water until al dente. Reserve 1/2 cup pasta water, then drain.
2. Heat olive oil in a pan. Sauté garlic until fragrant. Add clams and wine. Cover and cook until clams open.
3. Toss cooked linguine with the clams, adding reserved pasta water if needed. Garnish with parsley.

Tortellini in Brodo

Ingredients:

- 400g tortellini (meat or cheese-filled)
- 1.5L chicken or beef broth
- Parmesan cheese for serving
- Salt to taste

Instructions:

1. Bring the broth to a boil. Add tortellini and cook until tender.
2. Serve hot with grated Parmesan.

Fettuccine al Pesto Genovese

Ingredients:

- 400g fettuccine
- 100g fresh basil leaves
- 50g pine nuts
- 2 garlic cloves
- 100ml olive oil
- 50g Parmesan cheese, grated
- Salt and pepper to taste

Instructions:

1. Blend basil, pine nuts, garlic, olive oil, and Parmesan to make pesto. Season with salt and pepper.
2. Cook fettuccine in salted boiling water until al dente. Reserve 1/2 cup pasta water, then drain.
3. Toss pasta with pesto, using reserved pasta water to adjust consistency.

Orecchiette with Broccoli Rabe

Ingredients:

- 400g orecchiette
- 300g broccoli rabe, chopped
- 3 garlic cloves, minced
- 2 tbsp olive oil
- 1 tsp red chili flakes
- Salt and pepper to taste

Instructions:

1. Cook orecchiette in salted boiling water. Add broccoli rabe in the last 2 minutes. Reserve 1/2 cup pasta water, then drain.
2. Heat olive oil in a pan. Sauté garlic and chili flakes.
3. Toss orecchiette and broccoli rabe in the garlic oil. Adjust with reserved pasta water, season, and serve hot.

Cacio e Pepe

Ingredients:

- 400g spaghetti or tonnarelli
- 100g Pecorino Romano, finely grated
- 2 tsp freshly ground black pepper
- Salt for the pasta water

Instructions:

1. Cook pasta in salted boiling water until al dente. Reserve 1 cup pasta water, then drain.
2. Toast black pepper in a dry pan over medium heat. Add reserved pasta water to the pan and bring to a simmer.
3. Add the pasta and toss to coat. Gradually mix in Pecorino, stirring vigorously to create a creamy sauce. Serve immediately.

Rigatoni alla Norma

Ingredients:

- 400g rigatoni
- 1 large eggplant, diced
- 400g canned tomatoes
- 2 garlic cloves, minced
- 2 tbsp olive oil
- Fresh basil leaves
- Ricotta salata, grated
- Salt and pepper to taste

Instructions:

1. Cook rigatoni in salted boiling water until al dente. Drain.
2. Sauté eggplant in olive oil until golden. Remove and set aside.
3. In the same pan, cook garlic until fragrant, then add tomatoes. Simmer for 10 minutes.
4. Stir in the eggplant and basil. Toss with rigatoni and top with ricotta salata.

Fagottini di Pasta con Funghi

Ingredients:

- 400g fresh pasta sheets
- 200g mushrooms, finely chopped
- 1 shallot, minced
- 2 tbsp olive oil
- 100g ricotta cheese
- 100g Parmesan cheese, grated
- Salt and pepper to taste

Instructions:

1. Sauté mushrooms and shallots in olive oil until tender. Let cool, then mix with ricotta and Parmesan.
2. Cut pasta sheets into squares, place filling in the center, and fold into bundles.
3. Cook in salted boiling water until tender. Serve with melted butter or a light cream sauce.

Pasticcio di Maccheroni

Ingredients:

- 400g macaroni
- 300g Bolognese sauce
- 300ml béchamel sauce
- 150g mozzarella, shredded
- 50g Parmesan, grated

Instructions:

1. Cook macaroni until al dente. Preheat oven to 180°C (350°F).
2. Mix macaroni with Bolognese sauce and béchamel.
3. Transfer to a baking dish, top with mozzarella and Parmesan. Bake for 20–25 minutes until golden.

Spaghetti con Pomodorini e Basilico

Ingredients:

- 400g spaghetti
- 300g cherry tomatoes, halved
- 2 garlic cloves, minced
- 3 tbsp olive oil
- Fresh basil leaves
- Salt and pepper to taste

Instructions:

1. Cook spaghetti in salted boiling water until al dente. Reserve 1/2 cup pasta water, then drain.
2. Sauté garlic in olive oil until fragrant. Add tomatoes and cook until softened.
3. Toss spaghetti with the sauce, adding reserved pasta water as needed. Garnish with basil.

Farfalle with Lemon and Zucchini

Ingredients:

- 400g farfalle
- 2 zucchinis, thinly sliced
- Zest and juice of 1 lemon
- 2 tbsp olive oil
- 50g Parmesan, grated
- Salt and pepper to taste

Instructions:

1. Cook farfalle in salted boiling water until al dente. Reserve 1/2 cup pasta water, then drain.
2. Sauté zucchini in olive oil until tender. Add lemon zest and juice.
3. Toss farfalle with the zucchini mixture, Parmesan, and reserved pasta water. Season to taste.

Pappardelle with Porcini Mushrooms

Ingredients:

- 400g pappardelle
- 200g porcini mushrooms, sliced
- 2 garlic cloves, minced
- 2 tbsp olive oil
- 50ml heavy cream (optional)
- Fresh parsley, chopped
- Salt and pepper to taste

Instructions:

1. Cook pappardelle in salted boiling water until al dente. Drain.
2. Sauté garlic in olive oil, then add mushrooms and cook until tender. Stir in cream if using.
3. Toss pappardelle with the mushroom mixture and garnish with parsley.

Cannelloni with Ricotta and Spinach

Ingredients:

- 12 cannelloni tubes
- 300g ricotta cheese
- 300g spinach, cooked and chopped
- 400g tomato sauce
- 200ml béchamel sauce
- 50g Parmesan, grated

Instructions:

1. Mix ricotta and spinach. Stuff the mixture into cannelloni tubes.
2. Place tubes in a baking dish. Cover with tomato sauce, then béchamel. Top with Parmesan.
3. Bake at 180°C (350°F) for 25–30 minutes until golden and bubbling.

Spaghetti aglio, olio e peperoncino

Ingredients:

- 400g spaghetti
- 4 garlic cloves, thinly sliced
- 3 tbsp olive oil
- 2 red chili peppers, finely sliced
- Fresh parsley, chopped (optional)
- Salt for the pasta water

Instructions:

1. Cook spaghetti in salted boiling water until al dente. Reserve 1/2 cup pasta water, then drain.
2. Sauté garlic and chili in olive oil over medium heat until golden.
3. Toss the spaghetti in the pan, adding reserved pasta water to coat evenly. Garnish with parsley and serve.

Gnocchi alla Sorrentina

Ingredients:

- 500g potato gnocchi
- 400g tomato passata
- 150g mozzarella, diced
- 2 tbsp olive oil
- 2 garlic cloves, minced
- Fresh basil leaves
- Parmesan, grated

Instructions:

1. Cook gnocchi in boiling water until they float. Drain and set aside.
2. Sauté garlic in olive oil, then add tomato passata and simmer for 10 minutes. Stir in basil.
3. Toss gnocchi with the sauce and transfer to a baking dish. Top with mozzarella and Parmesan. Broil until bubbling.

Lasagna alla Caprese

Ingredients:

- 12 lasagna sheets
- 400g tomato sauce
- 300g mozzarella, sliced
- 150g ricotta cheese
- 100g Parmesan, grated
- Fresh basil leaves

Instructions:

1. Preheat oven to 180°C (350°F).
2. Layer lasagna sheets with tomato sauce, mozzarella, ricotta, and basil in a baking dish. Repeat layers.
3. Top with Parmesan and bake for 25–30 minutes until golden and bubbling.

Tagliatelle with Duck Ragù

Ingredients:

- 400g tagliatelle
- 300g duck meat, shredded
- 1 onion, diced
- 1 carrot, diced
- 2 celery stalks, diced
- 400ml red wine
- 2 tbsp olive oil
- Salt and pepper to taste

Instructions:

1. Sauté onion, carrot, and celery in olive oil until softened. Add duck meat and cook until browned.
2. Deglaze with red wine and simmer until reduced. Add a little water or stock if needed.
3. Cook tagliatelle until al dente, then toss with the ragù.

Ravioli al Nero di Seppia

Ingredients:

- 400g squid ink ravioli (store-bought or homemade)
- 300g shrimp, peeled and deveined
- 2 garlic cloves, minced
- 3 tbsp olive oil
- 100ml white wine
- Salt and pepper to taste

Instructions:

1. Cook ravioli in salted boiling water until tender. Drain and set aside.
2. Sauté garlic in olive oil, then add shrimp and cook until pink. Deglaze with white wine.
3. Toss ravioli in the pan with the shrimp sauce and serve.

Penne all'Amatriciana

Ingredients:

- 400g penne
- 150g guanciale or pancetta, diced
- 400g canned tomatoes
- 2 tbsp olive oil
- 50g Pecorino Romano, grated
- Salt and chili flakes to taste

Instructions:

1. Cook penne in salted boiling water until al dente. Drain.
2. Sauté guanciale in olive oil until crisp. Add tomatoes and chili flakes, simmer for 10 minutes.
3. Toss penne with the sauce and top with Pecorino Romano.

Fusilli with Sausage and Kale

Ingredients:

- 400g fusilli
- 200g Italian sausage, crumbled
- 150g kale, chopped
- 2 garlic cloves, minced
- 2 tbsp olive oil
- 50g Parmesan, grated

Instructions:

1. Cook fusilli in salted boiling water until al dente. Drain.
2. Sauté sausage in olive oil until browned. Add garlic and kale, cooking until wilted.
3. Toss fusilli with the sausage mixture and sprinkle with Parmesan.

Tagliatelle with Lobster and Saffron

Ingredients:

- 400g tagliatelle
- 2 lobster tails, cooked and chopped
- 1 garlic clove, minced
- 100ml heavy cream
- 1/4 tsp saffron threads
- 2 tbsp olive oil
- Salt and pepper to taste

Instructions:

1. Cook tagliatelle in salted boiling water until al dente. Drain.
2. Sauté garlic in olive oil, then add lobster. Stir in cream and saffron, cooking until thickened.
3. Toss tagliatelle with the lobster sauce and serve.

Spaghetti with Clams and Cherry Tomatoes

Ingredients:

- 400g spaghetti
- 500g fresh clams, cleaned
- 200g cherry tomatoes, halved
- 2 garlic cloves, minced
- 3 tbsp olive oil
- 1/2 cup white wine
- Fresh parsley, chopped

Instructions:

1. Cook spaghetti in salted boiling water until al dente. Drain.
2. Sauté garlic in olive oil, add clams and white wine. Cover and cook until clams open.
3. Add cherry tomatoes and simmer briefly. Toss with spaghetti and garnish with parsley.

Tortellini alla Panna

Ingredients:

- 400g cheese or meat tortellini
- 250ml heavy cream
- 2 tbsp butter
- 50g Parmesan, grated
- Salt and pepper to taste

Instructions:

1. Cook tortellini in salted boiling water until tender. Drain.
2. In a pan, melt butter, then stir in cream. Simmer until slightly thickened.
3. Toss tortellini with the sauce and sprinkle with Parmesan.

Tortellini with Mushroom Cream Sauce

Ingredients:

- 400g tortellini
- 200g mushrooms, sliced
- 2 garlic cloves, minced
- 250ml heavy cream
- 2 tbsp olive oil
- Salt and pepper to taste

Instructions:

1. Cook tortellini in salted boiling water until tender. Drain.
2. Sauté garlic and mushrooms in olive oil until browned. Add cream and simmer until thickened.
3. Toss tortellini in the sauce and serve.

Ziti al Forno with Sausage and Mozzarella

Ingredients:

- 400g ziti pasta
- 300g Italian sausage, crumbled
- 400g tomato sauce
- 200g mozzarella, diced
- 50g Parmesan, grated
- 2 tbsp olive oil

Instructions:

1. Preheat oven to 180°C (350°F). Cook ziti until al dente, then drain.
2. Brown sausage in olive oil, add tomato sauce and simmer.
3. Mix pasta with sauce and half the mozzarella. Transfer to a baking dish, top with remaining mozzarella and Parmesan. Bake until golden.

Spaghetti alla Puttanesca

Ingredients:

- 400g spaghetti
- 2 garlic cloves, minced
- 4 anchovy fillets, chopped
- 200g canned tomatoes
- 50g black olives, sliced
- 1 tbsp capers
- 3 tbsp olive oil

Instructions:

1. Cook spaghetti in salted water until al dente. Drain.
2. Sauté garlic and anchovies in olive oil, add tomatoes, olives, and capers. Simmer briefly.
3. Toss spaghetti with the sauce and serve.

Ravioli with Brown Butter and Sage

Ingredients:

- 400g ravioli
- 100g butter
- 8 fresh sage leaves
- Salt and pepper to taste
- Parmesan, grated

Instructions:

1. Cook ravioli in salted boiling water until tender. Drain.
2. Melt butter in a pan over medium heat, add sage leaves and cook until butter browns.
3. Toss ravioli in the brown butter and serve with Parmesan.

Gnocchi with Gorgonzola Sauce

Ingredients:

- 500g potato gnocchi
- 150g Gorgonzola cheese
- 200ml heavy cream
- 2 tbsp butter
- Salt and pepper to taste

Instructions:

1. Cook gnocchi in boiling water until they float. Drain.
2. Melt butter, add cream and Gorgonzola. Stir until cheese melts.
3. Toss gnocchi in the sauce and serve immediately.

Linguine with Scallops and Lemon

Ingredients:

- 400g linguine
- 300g scallops
- 2 garlic cloves, minced
- Zest and juice of 1 lemon
- 3 tbsp olive oil
- Fresh parsley, chopped

Instructions:

1. Cook linguine in salted boiling water until al dente. Drain.
2. Sear scallops in olive oil until golden. Remove and set aside.
3. Sauté garlic, add lemon juice and zest, then toss linguine in the sauce. Top with scallops and parsley.

Pappardelle with Truffle Cream Sauce

Ingredients:

- 400g pappardelle
- 250ml heavy cream
- 2 tbsp truffle oil
- 50g Parmesan, grated
- Salt and pepper to taste
- Fresh parsley, chopped

Instructions:

1. Cook pappardelle in salted water until al dente. Drain.
2. Heat cream in a pan, stir in truffle oil and Parmesan. Simmer until thickened.
3. Toss pasta in the sauce, season, and garnish with parsley.

Risotto alla Milanese with Pasta

Ingredients:

- 400g short pasta (e.g., orzo or ditalini)
- 1 small onion, minced
- 50g butter
- 1 pinch saffron threads, dissolved in 2 tbsp warm water
- 1/2 cup white wine
- 1L chicken stock
- 50g Parmesan, grated

Instructions:

1. Sauté onion in butter until softened. Add pasta and toast lightly.
2. Stir in wine, saffron, and stock gradually, cooking until pasta is al dente.
3. Mix in Parmesan and serve hot.

Penne alla Puttanesca

Ingredients:

- 400g penne
- 2 garlic cloves, minced
- 4 anchovy fillets, chopped
- 200g canned tomatoes
- 50g black olives, sliced
- 1 tbsp capers
- 3 tbsp olive oil

Instructions:

1. Cook penne in salted water until al dente. Drain.
2. Sauté garlic and anchovies in olive oil. Add tomatoes, olives, and capers. Simmer.
3. Toss penne with the sauce and serve.

Bucatini all'Amatriciana

Ingredients:

- 400g bucatini
- 100g guanciale or pancetta, diced
- 1 small onion, minced
- 200g canned tomatoes
- 50g Pecorino Romano, grated
- 2 tbsp olive oil

Instructions:

1. Cook bucatini in salted water until al dente. Drain.
2. Sauté guanciale and onion in olive oil until golden. Add tomatoes and simmer.
3. Toss bucatini with the sauce and sprinkle with Pecorino.

Fettuccine with Shrimp and Asparagus

Ingredients:

- 400g fettuccine
- 300g shrimp, peeled
- 200g asparagus, cut into 2-inch pieces
- 2 garlic cloves, minced
- 3 tbsp olive oil
- Zest and juice of 1 lemon

Instructions:

1. Cook fettuccine in salted water until al dente. Drain.
2. Sauté shrimp, asparagus, and garlic in olive oil. Add lemon zest and juice.
3. Toss fettuccine in the mixture and serve.

Orecchiette with Sausage and Broccoli

Ingredients:

- 400g orecchiette
- 300g Italian sausage, crumbled
- 200g broccoli florets
- 2 garlic cloves, minced
- 3 tbsp olive oil
- Parmesan, grated

Instructions:

1. Cook orecchiette and broccoli together in salted water until pasta is al dente. Drain.
2. Brown sausage in olive oil, add garlic. Toss with pasta and broccoli.
3. Serve with Parmesan.

Ravioli with Butternut Squash

Ingredients:

- 400g butternut squash ravioli
- 100g butter
- 6 fresh sage leaves
- 50g Parmesan, grated

Instructions:

1. Cook ravioli in salted boiling water until tender. Drain.
2. Melt butter, add sage leaves, and cook until butter is browned.
3. Toss ravioli in the brown butter and serve with Parmesan.

Cavatelli with Sweet Potatoes and Brown Butter

Ingredients:

- 400g cavatelli
- 200g sweet potatoes, diced and roasted
- 100g butter
- 6 sage leaves
- Salt and pepper to taste

Instructions:

1. Cook cavatelli in salted water until al dente. Drain.
2. Melt butter, add sage, and cook until browned. Mix in roasted sweet potatoes.
3. Toss cavatelli with the mixture and serve.

Spaghetti alle Vongole Veraci

Ingredients:

- 400g spaghetti
- 500g fresh clams (vongole veraci), cleaned
- 2 garlic cloves, minced
- 2 tbsp olive oil
- 1/2 cup white wine
- Fresh parsley, chopped
- Lemon zest

Instructions:

1. Cook spaghetti in salted boiling water until al dente. Drain.
2. Sauté garlic in olive oil, add clams and white wine, cover, and cook until clams open.
3. Toss pasta with clams and sauce, garnish with parsley and lemon zest.

Agnolotti with Braised Beef

Ingredients:

- 400g agnolotti pasta
- 300g braised beef, shredded
- 1 onion, minced
- 1 carrot, minced
- 1 celery stalk, minced
- 1 cup beef broth
- 2 tbsp olive oil
- 50g Parmesan, grated

Instructions:

1. Cook agnolotti in salted boiling water until tender. Drain.
2. Sauté onion, carrot, and celery in olive oil until softened. Add shredded beef and broth, simmer until the liquid reduces.
3. Toss agnolotti with beef mixture, sprinkle with Parmesan, and serve.

Tortellini with Parmesan Broth

Ingredients:

- 400g tortellini (cheese or meat-filled)
- 1L homemade or store-bought Parmesan broth
- Fresh parsley, chopped
- Parmesan, grated for serving

Instructions:

1. Heat the Parmesan broth in a large pot.
2. Cook tortellini in boiling salted water until tender, then add to the hot broth.
3. Serve with chopped parsley and grated Parmesan.

Tagliolini with Anchovies and Capers

Ingredients:

- 400g tagliolini
- 4 anchovy fillets, chopped
- 1 tbsp capers
- 2 garlic cloves, minced
- 3 tbsp olive oil
- Fresh parsley, chopped
- Zest of 1 lemon

Instructions:

1. Cook tagliolini in salted boiling water until al dente. Drain.
2. Sauté garlic, anchovies, and capers in olive oil until fragrant.
3. Toss pasta in the mixture, garnish with parsley and lemon zest.

Lasagna di Pesce

Ingredients:

- 400g lasagna sheets
- 500g mixed fish (e.g., cod, salmon), flaked
- 200g shrimp, peeled and chopped
- 200g ricotta cheese
- 1L white wine and fish stock blend
- 2 tbsp olive oil
- Fresh dill, chopped

Instructions:

1. Preheat oven to 180°C (350°F).
2. Cook lasagna sheets in salted boiling water until tender. Drain.
3. Sauté seafood in olive oil, add ricotta and a little stock, and mix. Layer pasta, seafood, and stock mixture in a baking dish. Bake until golden.
4. Garnish with fresh dill.

Pappardelle with Veal Ragù

Ingredients:

- 400g pappardelle
- 500g veal shoulder, cubed
- 1 onion, chopped
- 2 garlic cloves, minced
- 1 carrot, minced
- 1 cup red wine
- 2 cups tomato sauce
- 2 tbsp olive oil
- Fresh rosemary

Instructions:

1. Cook pappardelle in salted boiling water until al dente. Drain.
2. Brown veal in olive oil, then sauté garlic, onion, and carrot. Add wine and simmer until reduced.
3. Add tomato sauce, rosemary, and cook until the sauce thickens. Toss pasta with ragù and serve.

www.ingramcontent.com/pod-product-compliance
Lightning Source LLC
LaVergne TN
LVHW081500060526
838201LV00056BA/2856